Arctic Wolves

by Betsy Rathburn

BLASTOFF!
READERS
2

BELLWETHER MEDIA · MINNEAPOLIS, MN

Blastoff! Readers are carefully developed by literacy experts to build reading stamina and move students toward fluency by combining standards-based content with developmentally appropriate text.

Level 1 provides the most support through repetition of high-frequency words, light text, predictable sentence patterns, and strong visual support.

Level 2 offers early readers a bit more challenge through varied sentences, increased text load, and text-supportive special features.

Level 3 advances early-fluent readers toward fluency through increased text load, less reliance on photos, advancing concepts, longer sentences, and more complex special features.

LEVELS

★ **Blastoff! Universe**

Reading Level

BLASTOFF! Beginners — Grade K

BLASTOFF! READERS — Grades 1–3

BLASTOFF! DISCOVERY — Grade 4

This edition first published in 2021 by Bellwether Media, Inc.

No part of this publication may be reproduced in whole or in part without written permission of the publisher. For information regarding permission, write to Bellwether Media, Inc., Attention: Permissions Department, 6012 Blue Circle Drive, Minnetonka, MN 55343.

Library of Congress Cataloging-in-Publication Data

Names: Rathburn, Betsy, author.
Title: Arctic wolves / by Betsy Rathburn.
Description: Minneapolis, MN : Bellwether Media, Inc., 2021. | Series: Blast off! readers: animals of the Arctic | Includes bibliographical references and index. | Audience: Ages 5-8 | Audience: Grades K-1 | Summary: "Relevant images match informative text in this introduction to Arctic wolves. Intended for students in kindergarten through third grade"-- Provided by publisher.
Identifiers: LCCN 2019053863 (print) | LCCN 2019053864 (ebook) | ISBN 9781644872116 (library binding) | ISBN 9781618919694 (ebook)
Subjects: LCSH: Gray wolf--Juvenile literature. | Zoology--Arctic regions--Juvenile literature.
Classification: LCC QL737.C22 R389 2021 (print) | LCC QL737.C22 (ebook) | DDC 599.7730911/3--dc23
LC record available at https://lccn.loc.gov/2019053863
LC ebook record available at https://lccn.loc.gov/2019053864

Editor: Kieran Downs   Designer: Brittany McIntosh

Printed in the United States of America, North Mankato, MN

Table of Contents

Life in the Arctic

Arctic wolves **thrive** in the Arctic **biome**! These **mammals** have **adapted** to become top hunters.

4

They roam northern
Canada and Greenland.

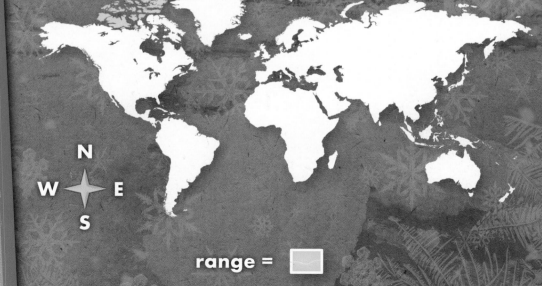

Arctic Wolf Range

N
W E
S

range =

5

The Arctic **tundra** is cold and snowy. Arctic wolves have two layers of fur. These help the wolves stay warm.

The white color helps the wolves stay hidden!

Furry paws also keep Arctic wolves warm. They can walk across cold ground easily.

Special Adaptations

small ears

two layers of fur

bushy tail

furry paws

Their fur-covered paws also help Arctic wolves **grip** slippery ice!

9

Arctic wolves have small ears. This is because smaller body parts lose less heat.

The wolves curl up to sleep. **Bushy** tails keep their bare noses warm!

Howling for Help

Arctic wolves stick together to survive. **Packs** travel together to find food.

When they rest, the wolves snuggle together to keep warm.

pack

Arctic wolves talk to each other. They **howl** to find their packs.

14

They call for help when enemies
are close. Arctic wolves fight
enemies as a pack!

The Arctic has frozen ground. It is hard to dig **dens**.

Arctic wolves search for rock caves and shallow holes. Wolves and their **pups** stay warm!

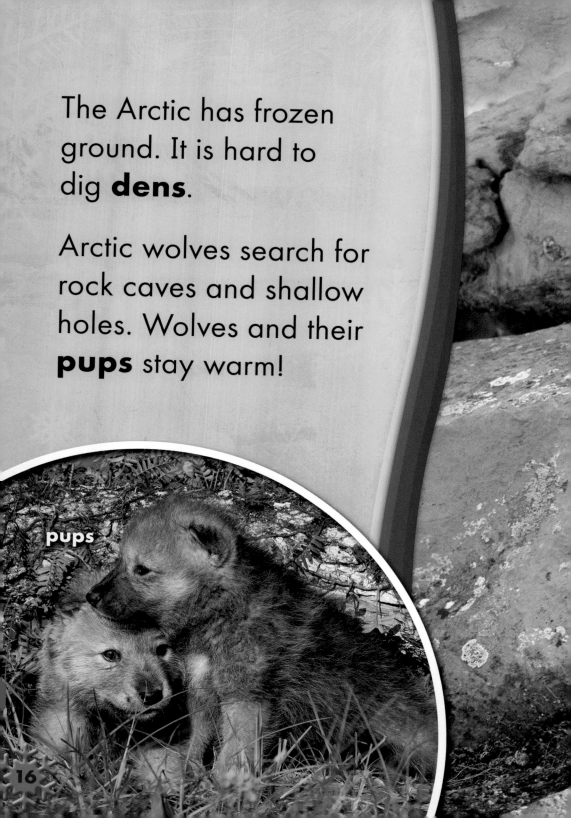

pups

Arctic Wolf Stats

Least Concern	Near Threatened	Vulnerable	Endangered	Critically Endangered	Extinct in the Wild	Extinct

conservation status: least concern

life span: up to 10 years

den

17

Hunters on the Move

Arctic wolves work together to hunt. They take down large animals!

They often travel with **prey**. They follow caribou to warmer weather.

Arctic Wolf Diet

muskoxen

caribou

Arctic hares

19

Arctic wolves work alone to hunt small animals. Strong, sharp teeth help the wolves tear apart prey.

These **predators** are
Arctic survivors!

Glossary

adapted—changed over a long period of time

biome—a large area with certain plants, animals, and weather

bushy—thick and furry

dens—sheltered places

grip—to hold tightly

howl—to let out a long, loud cry

mammals—warm-blooded animals that have backbones and feed their young milk

packs—groups of wolves that live and hunt together

predators—animals that hunt other animals for food

prey—animals that are hunted by other animals for food

pups—baby Arctic wolves

thrive—to grow well

tundra—rocky land in the Arctic that has a frozen layer

To Learn More

AT THE LIBRARY

Albertson, Al. *Gray Wolves.* Minneapolis, Minn.: Bellwether Media, 2020.

Cocca, Lisa Colozza. *Tundra Animals.* Vero Beach, Fla.: Rourke Educational Media, 2019.

Pettiford, Rebecca. *Arctic Foxes.* Minneapolis, Minn.: Bellwether Media, 2019.

ON THE WEB

FACTSURFER

Factsurfer.com gives you a safe, fun way to find more information.

1. Go to www.factsurfer.com.

2. Enter "Arctic wolves" into the search box and click 🔍.

3. Select your book cover to see a list of related content.

Index

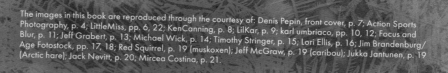

The images in this book are reproduced through the courtesy of: Denis Pepin, front cover, p. 7; Action Sports Photography, p. 4; LittleMiss, pp. 6, 22; KenCanning, p. 8; LilKar, p. 9; karl umbriaco, pp. 10, 12; Focus and Blur, p. 11; Jeff Grabert, p. 13; Michael Wick, p. 14; Timothy Stringer, p. 15; Lori Ellis, p. 16; Jim Brandenburg/ Age Fotostock, pp. 17, 18; Red Squirrel, p. 19 (muskoxen); Jeff McGraw, p. 19 (caribou); Jukka Jantunen, p. 19 (Arctic hare); Jack Nevitt, p. 20; Mircea Costina, p. 21.

24